ANALYZING AND UNDERSTANDING WEEKLY FINANCIAL NEWS

ANALYZING AND UNDERSTANDING WEEKLY FINANCIAL NEWS

A Comprehensive Guide

RWG PUBLISHING

RWG Publishing

CONTENTS

First Printing, 2024

CHAPTER 1

Introduction to Financial News Recap

With an increase in readers globally and increased access to content, traditional news sources should be able to perform satisfactorily. Newswire agencies do change wires to numerous subscribing exchange centers. The comparatively high time in making a large portion of financial news and less than instantaneous dissemination on the Internet give a great opportunity for all subscribers to access news that will influence price volume and volatility of financial products. Because after real-time data, they require instantaneous attention. An aggregator that combines articles from various news sources is also known to analyzable vassals.

Various online sources provide an excellent channel for access to financial news. Among these available resources, there are real-time newswire services. Some of these newswire sources distribute news that moves markets instantly, such as Bloomberg, Reuters, and Dow Jones Newswires, in no less than 18 languages. At the same time, real-time news is only available for a limited number of financial decision makers. TV and radio channels also dedicate daily programs to report financial news. In reporting on finances, most magazines and local newspapers keep a few hours before publishing time. Henceforth, financial news is based on very slow information.

Importance of Staying Informed

Moreover, skimming through top-tier newspapers will not suffice. Traders need to read the financial sections of national and international newspapers carefully in order to analyze the articles, form an opinion, and translate this into a market strategy. And, out of total confusion, they must understand the importance and underlying relevance of those news items that move the markets. Simply scanning through the headlines would not be enough. In the newspapers, avoid consumer news, which deals with indices and releases already known to the market, and company press releases, useless when trying to learn something new. Unfortunately, information is not free. The good material from the international newspapers and websites is rather expensive. We analyze news from a variety of sources: newspapers, newswires, business magazines, and economic journals are all rifled through for usable information. Remember that market-moving news is what everyone is talking about, and not what is reported in specialized but ignored magazines. Crises are not only peculiar because they create relevant news, but also because readers are stranded on the island of perfect information.

To succeed in this business, traders and managers must be well-informed. Financial markets are constantly in motion, 24 hours a day, around the globe. What happens at night in Japan can affect our stock prices the following trading day. We rely on a multitude of daily newspapers and periodicals, websites, and TV channels. Bloomberg terminals are present on virtually every trading desk. With the constant deluge of financial news available from a myriad of sources, there is no lack of reading material. Yet, haven't you found yourself asked to comment on a news item that you had not heard of before, implying that the market knew more than you did? With all the news, readers cannot possibly keep up-to-date about everything.

Benefits of Weekly Recaps

Over the last months, I have gotten several such recaps from collaborators and I could see the great value they were receiving from such a service. As a result, the idea came to my mind that my weekly newsletter subscribers would probably like to receive a recap such as the one they were doing, for all news sources that I am scraping.

Reading a weekly financial news recap has multiple benefits. First and foremost, reading a weekly recap could save you a lot of time - for example, you could read the weekly recap over the weekend and during the following week you could dedicate your time to other important activities. Secondly, due to the limited time that major news recaps have, they tend to focus on the most important news of the week and the news items that were most likely to affect the daily lives of the population, while filtering out the noise. Thirdly, you are receiving information from multiple sources, as I mentioned earlier, without the need to visit each individual one. Finally, you are able to understand and recognize quickly the important news items of the week. Scientists call this 'information with as little effort as possible'.

CHAPTER 2

Key Concepts in Financial News

Finance is a field focusing on time, value, and risk. In layman's terms, this means that when we're looking at finance, we're either looking back at how money was spent in the past, analyzing where to put our future savings, or examining how to manage risks. As such, the connotations of language used in financial contexts are often emotional and political as well as technical. This happens because the value of a financial product or instrument usually reflects a set of beliefs and expectations and thus can be subject to manipulation and opportunistic behavior. The news accompanying this kind of events often reflects those emotions and opinions. As financial research is becoming more data-driven, this comprehensive guide intends to help readers in understanding the news.

Market Trends and Analysis

Our research is different from the previous research, as we also examine the effect of article content by analyzing the article text to extract common market trends and analyses. By identifying common market trends and analyses, we can inform the information aggregation system to include financial articles that are relevant to these common market trends and analyses. The basis for identifying common market trends and analyses is the idea that some phrases appear consistently in similar contexts in a group of related financial articles. Therefore, our article contains two different studies: the study of an information aggregation system, and the study of common market trends and analyses from text. Our article focuses on the second study. To the best of our knowledge, our research is the first to analyze financial news to produce common market trends and analyses.

The most common and basic form of extracting features from a given financial text is probably market trends and analysis. Typically, market trends and analyses are related to one or more entities. A lot of NLP and IR works have been developed to extract market trends and analyses from large quantities of online financial news. A typical setting for such research is where an information aggregation system first selects a given set of financial documents dealing with some financial entity, and then a subsequent analysis module processes this set of documents to identify market trends and analyses. The individual articles have been found to contain similar findings to the previous work.

Economic Indicators

Countless pieces of financial research have found a link between past movements in asset returns and scheduled information releases. That link is the basis for the institutional structure of financial news - why it is viewed as important. Revisions to economic indicators of many types are released at scheduled times. Moreover, those revisions are thought relevant to the decision making of households and firms. And, noise in the monthly estimates keep professional macroeconomic forecasters in great demand and are the foundation for a discipline of financial economists exploiting those same features. A massive surveillance mechanism by traditional macro economists keeps advancing as they are able to use the same data to examine relations to asset returns that they used to ignore. Weekly high frequency macroeconomic indicators are neither revised from their initial estimate nor subjected to pooling of cross sectional observations. Weekly indicators provide an alternative to using returns on the most important proxies for an event study methodologies' critical assumption - asset prices respond only to information revealed at the scheduled release time of the indicator.

CHAPTER 3

Tools and Platforms for Accessing Financial News

The professionalism and expertise required to gather this vast quantity of news information have accumulated over several years. At the beginning of the project in 2015, we sought the direct help of a professional financial news analysis and distribution service that operated through a Graphical User Interface (GUI) platform enabling journalists to select the specific news they wanted to monitor. Unfortunately, at the time, the newsfeed company could not provide built-in tools with formats that fit our requirements for data collection. Although I took note of the news sources mentioned by the professional operator, it took getting my hands dirty and navigating through online financial news aggregators and websites to discover the best platforms to gather the data.

The compilation of the weekly financial news is an exhaustive process and requires the navigational expertise of many online platforms to gather the news. The platforms include search engines and advanced search tools, direct access to websites of professional financial news organizations, custom scrapers on the websites of general news publications, and news aggregators. The project also relies on financial data vendors to download the fingerprint security prices and returns from the various stock and bond markets worldwide.

Online Sources

In summary, although gathering data from different sources (e.g., news, Internet, and ticker tape) is necessary, the relevance, completeness, and accuracy of the data must be addressed. Specifically, a comprehensive check is required to ensure that two news databases are consistent in terms of content and coverage, especially when one database is used to tag positive and negative news, and the other one is used for content analysis. In the case of the Internet, many newspapers are creating net websites that allow their subscribers to read the full text of the daily and weekly newspaper business coverage. The press releases from the net are also available. News sources via the net websites include The New York Times, The Wall Street Journal, San Jose Mercury News, etc. Popular financial news services, such as Zacks, Baseline and Market Guide, provide updates and announcements (accruals, changes in accounting policies, etc.) via the Internet.

Presently, many newspapers have their printed edition available online. A few well-known online sources are The Wall Street Journal, The New York Times, The Los Angeles Times, The Washington Post, The Chicago Tribune, The Boston Globe, The San Francisco Chronicle, and Toronto Globe and Mail. Online newspapers that are freely available are The Daily Telegraph, Nikkei Net, Frankfurter Zeitung, Hong Kong Standard, and China Times. Financial services provided by financial news firms are also available online. These services range from general economic news such as Bloomberg to more specialized news such as News CAP from Bridge Information Systems, NIKKEI QUICK NEWS, and AFP World Wide Service.

Other potentially useful sites are newswires from Reuters, Dow Jones, Knight-Ridder, and AP.

Mobile Applications

First, the newspapers. Most major newspapers with significant financial sections have mobile versions of each of their news stories. The larger newspapers like the Wall Street Journal, the Financial Times, and the New York Times have excellent mobile websites as well as mobile applications. Countless other papers of lesser pedigree also offer their wares on the mobile web. There are also a number of excellent multi-paper news resources that offer access through a single application.

Until fairly recently, one had to be a big bank or a rich financial investor in order to get access to important financial news as soon as it is released. In a global market, minutes really can mean the difference between making or losing a lot of money. Thankfully, with the proliferation of smart mobile communications devices, this is no longer the case. First, most newspapers and news organizations offer mobile versions of their web portals. Second, a number of specialized mobile applications are available. We review both here.

CHAPTER 4

Interpreting Financial Data

A very powerful tool in understanding the fundamental financial data is something called the forward rate. This is the rate you would use to establish future interest rates. This is a very important tool if you want to lock a fixed return on your investment for a period in the future. You can use this tool to extend bond investing to international markets. If you are able to establish an interest rate risk exposure and you don't want to sell the bond, then you can buy or sell some other financial instrument that will balance your portfolio and give you the interest rate return. Using these tools associated with interest rates, you can expand the range of fixed income investments in your portfolio.

In discussing any financial topic, a solid understanding of the basic statistical concepts is crucial. Every day we are bombarded with seemingly important financial statistics. Using the skill set introduced here, not only will you be able to interpret the meaning and quality of these statistics, but also you will be able to be fluent in the language that will give meaning and add value to financial forecasts and decisions additionally. These concepts provide tools for summarizing and describing the important news in the daily financial press.

Reading Stock Charts

We provide a general overview of a stock chart to familiarize with the representation. This knowledge is useful to understand the markets and other terminologies such as market timing. Market timing is the ability of a trader to make a directional prediction either up or down depending upon his knowledge of the price action. The notion of random walk in the stock market comes in part from the fact that stock prices seem to evolve with new news and/or revelation of patterns that are characterized as noisy. Although stock prices are said to evolve completely with new news, both periods of stability and gains and periods of instability and negative returns are observed. The efficiency issue has been widely discussed in the early work of Mandelbrot.

Stock charts capture the historical patterns of the stock performance and are used by traders to decide on the stock price action and to make profitable decisions. There are various patterns in stock charts, some of which have interesting implications for investors. These patterns typically unveil the overall performance of the stock and are often useful to know the stock progress. The date reactivity of the different traders also shapes the formation of these patterns.

Understanding Financial Jargon

In our newspaper corpus, 12% of the words are in the financial jargon. In the one corpus of the news articles indexed by the Financial Times in 1989, the rate is even as high as 16%. This shows that financial jargon is indeed frequent in the financial news articles. Being partially equipped with financial knowledge in early months, we also realized that understanding financial jargon can be very tricky, especially when the jargon is the key topic of the week. For example, 'equity' may have different meanings in different articles than Newton's laws' in a physics class or 'stock' in a supermarket. Therefore, besides the issue of working with concepts and understanding financial news, we are also interested in the issue of understanding financial jargon in the articles we are given. In this section, we present our techniques for understanding financial jargon, which are also taken advantage of by our event-driven system.

CHAPTER 5

Impact of Major Events on Financial Markets

Aside from generic news such as those from the Wall Street Journal, there are also specialized financial news media such as Bloomberg, the Financial Times, Thomson Reuters and others. Financial blogs such as Zero Hedge and financial expert videos such as those from CNBC, can influence the market as well. Many trading and investment firms also provide strategy notes and these have utmost importance. Estimated market indices such as the Consumer Price Index (CPI) may have an impact.

We have seen different types of information summarization methods in one of the previous sections, Wall Street Horizon. This section deals with news that affects financial markets. In most cases, major global events such as economic, political, social, and financial events, create news and then it impacts further economic activities. To study this cause-effect relationship, we have to assess the impact of news from different sources on financial markets where it includes stock price, financial volume, volatility, and others. Experimental analytics on this are carried out with datasets from numerous domains such as stock markets, financial news, Web search, and others. Surely, when more news sources are combined, the analytics becomes powerful. By now, text analysis tools and platforms such as NLTK, OpenNLP, Stanford CoreNLP, AlchemyAPI and WordNet are powerful enough to handle various big financial and news data.

Geopolitical Events

Geopolitical events and factors encompass: (a) wars, (b) international conflicts, (c) diplomatic agreements and other negotiations, (d) political revolutions and revolts, (e) political crises and changes, (f) actions against and related to terrorist groups, (g) incidents and disputes in oceans and seas, (h) political parties and international relations-related statements, (i) decisions and statements from major official organizations such as the UN, the WTO, NATO, NAFTA, and others, (j) interventions and invasions by foreign countries or, more generally, foreign interference with financial impacts, (k) actions related to national security, (l) confrontational declarations, (m) important events in countries such as elections, mergers, acquisitions, privatizations, nationalizations, and licenses, (n) discoveries in oil-oriented countries, but also (o) other forms of instability, either similar to the points just highlighted or different.

Geopolitical events related to international politics and global affairs can have substantial immediate and long-term impacts on financial markets. They can exacerbate or further dim the outlook of a region or a country, have serious impacts on the value of currency across multiple jurisdictions, increase the price of commodities relevant either to a region or to large portions of the world, contribute to shaping up the inflationary outlook of several economies, and impact monetary policy decisions, among others. It is essential to understand not only the components of geopolitics but also the broader geopolitical narration that accompanies them.

Natural Disasters

One main event that can bias sample analysis and affect market reaction is a natural disaster. There are many different types of disasters: earthquake, flood, terrorist attacks, hurricanes, and governmental human-made disasters, among others, that have occurred within the last decade. These disasters have caused a significant level of economic damage and more unexpected minus expected components in national income measures. There are different degrees in terms of damage caused by such disasters and government responses to provide relief. Governments act fast in cases of war or earthquakes because there are reduced costs in providing relief in such cases. It is less expensive to help these injured victims. Rescue and relief activities may include the opening of active arenas in which further rescues can be made easily. Restoring disrupted transportation is another possible effort. Governments may also carry out fiscal expansion to restore the economies and to compensate for the damage imposed by these natural disasters. This analysis suggests that negative movements in the crisis event time variables have a different time course. In some cases, there are natural and human-made disaster crises that can be either short-lived, but in all cases, the crises are less likely to result in a reduced event time.

CHAPTER 6

Strategies for Making Informed Decisions

Another piece of supporting evidence is that good news is somewhat less likely to be fully incorporated into market outcomes than bad news. For example, no beta is associated with news of earnings losses, and bond market reaction appears to be stronger to business misconduct losses than to equivalent good news earnings surprises. It seems that the market is biased against firms with a history of bad news, and that bad news firms may actually have better stock returns on an equal footing. This is the same effect observed during financial market booms and busts. In markets without any sort of dividend effects, stock price peaks expectedly coincide with heavy decumulation of surplus as investors buy stocks in order to participate in a rise in prices. However, during market downturns, most of the selling comes from investors liquidizing their holdings. Adult investors, mutual funds, insurance companies, and business trusts are rarely observed to repatriate receipts. Instead, they sell their holdings to change their asset mix. The recent market downturn and the

16-year-old market history of financial markets accurately provide us with substantial empirical results.

Research results very strongly support the view that the stock market is much more sensitive to negative news than to positive news. Negative news events studied by financial researchers have included announcements of financial distress, financial reorganization, and exchange delisting, earnings losses, and losses due to business misconduct. These types of negative news tend to be expected to lead to a decrease in stock price, and researchers observe that the results support this expectation. Positive news events have included announcements of profits, stock splits, and being called from a bond issue. However, the announcement of positive news has a much smaller effect on the price of a stock than negative news. This evidence is consistent with the popular belief that bad news travels fast.

Finally, it is important to remember that the news is not just a current reflection of current events. Rather, it is more important to focus on the future. The value of the news only exists if it provides an outside view as to what will happen in the future. An investor needs to know what actions other people will perform if the investor wants to respond to these actions. If the news spreads some bad information about a firm (for example, that the firm will be sued for product liability or that it will release very bad financial results in the near future), then the stock price should go down, and the investor should sell the stock. It is only when the news provides an unbiased and accurate source of information about the future that it can command such an impact.

While reading the news, it is important to notice and keep track of what is being presented in the newspapers regularly. Is the news always about the same topic? If the topics are always changing, will these changes in the presented news influence the market? Will the presence of these articles in the newspapers cause firms to react, and will they become news events?

Risk Management Techniques

In our context, the problem of financial health is understood as the possibility that a given bank balance might become negative in the near future and within a given period. Risk management lends one the ability to predict the individual or combined effects of investment decisions on a business and to be prepared to deal with the implications. Over the last year, there has been some interest in the merging of news articles and financial data or models. Banks in the US are heavily regulated, and the use of those news articles can be of interest to FED-like governments.

Risk management is an activity that involves identifying, assessing, controlling, and mitigating risks to an organization. The aim is to minimize the negative effects of risks and capitalize on the benefits associated with opportunities. Total risk management capitalizes on both opportunities and difficult situations. Risk management is concerned with the identification of potential problems that might arise in specific investment requisition-investment and the initiation of actions to alleviate or "hedge" the potential impact of these problems.

Investment Diversification

There are many different types of mutual funds or investment products that one can invest in. One can select a different investment strategy like investing in large-cap stocks, investing in small-cap stocks, or in stocks of specific sectors. Large-cap stocks, as the name suggests, represent companies that are large in size. Large-cap funds invest in stocks of such companies and have a good track record of paying dividends. While small-cap companies are known to be smaller and thus have more growth potential. Small-cap funds invest in the stocks of such smaller companies. Scientists and researchers have shown that small-cap companies perform better than large-cap companies over the long term.

Diversification is a simple investment strategy. Rather than placing all of your money in one stock, you spread out your investment over a large number of stocks. If one stock goes down in value, then other stocks will hopefully go up. If you have invested in a diversified way, then the overall effect of one stock going down will not be as significant. Investors have been investing in mutual funds to obtain the benefits of diversification. Professional fund managers do the job of buying and selling different equities, ensuring investors that their money is invested not only in many unique stocks but also in a wide range of sectors.

CHAPTER 7

Ethical Considerations in Financial Reporting

Many businesses and other business organizations stand accused of actions harmful to investors, employees, customers, the communities they impact, and consumers of their goods, services, and commodities. Our principal concern is with financial reporting, defined broadly to include that information provided to shareholders and creditors beyond the annual report and annual report preparation process, and the information made available to other stakeholders about the financial objective and performance of a business organization. Since the performance of a business organization should acknowledge the effects on other stakeholders, the broadness of our concern with financial reporting is justified. The concern extends beyond formal legal requirements or what is determined by technical accounting and financial phenomenon. Since businesses might take actions that will harm a variety of constituents, the information shared with various constituents should extend beyond formal, legal, and computer-based confidence-inspiring information such as sales-growth trends or stock price. Our guide is structured around the question of what users of financial statements should know about credible information. We have made the role and ethical behavior of users of financial information and the need for information that can be relied on to minimize harmful economic activity or stopping the financing of a business.

Protocols and rules have been in existence for decades, largely designed to manage the activities of business organizations, the institutions of civil society, and political organizations. The potential of business, especially global corporations, to inflict both direct and indirect harm has raised the question of the duty of business to do no harm or, for a larger ideal, to contribute to human welfare. Businesses cannot honor this principle without being transparent in their business activities and accountable for the decisions and other activities they pursue.

CHAPTER 8

The Future of Financial News

Over the centuries, diplomatic codes, market corners, and trading monopolies have extracted payment for valuable information through the imposition of taxes, predial duties, traducing mysteries, and monopolies. Tradable information anyone can find is of little value. Attack and defense should be waged against secrets, and we should not be surprised that successful attacks devalue that which they defeat, reduce the borders of the hidden jungle land. There are too many sources of information, acting as arbiters of the hour's importance and priority. Instead, it's an arena of psychology on which rewards or penalties are imposed without uniformity of voices or considerations. But psychology is but a game, something for skillful traders who are experts and milk others for whatever reason, goofs, or whims. Actually, the news must lead to the rethinking about the importance or future weighting in the future of factors not currently part of the known equation which the pros are using. Using the known as a known, decided in advance with decisions contingent upon expectations, it isn't even keeping the safeguarding.

The daily newspapers that are now downscaling and broadcasting their financial data were, in their heyday, the main sources of such data. Looking into further developments at the level of the mass media and at the level of individuals and organizations that consume financial data but are not professional receivers or producers of the same, two questions arise: Will the current "wall of worry" improve in the short term, and will long-term development follow the secular downward trend? If capacity problems were the driving force, it is wiser to conclude that there will be an improvement in the short term, and perhaps things will get even better over the longer term. If, however, the issue is cost structure, then shake-ups and compressions could only produce price scars: large organizations - corporations and governments - will create their trading pit to enlarge their own view, while retail customers are supplied only with marginal, low-quality services.

Emerging Technologies

Recent advances in artificial intelligence applications—especially in NLP—can help the financial industry analyze large amounts of textual data. Language models, deep learning models, or transformer-based models that understand and generate human language, such as BERT, XLNet, or T5, can be used to extract useful information from financial text. These unconventional NLP techniques can also be combined with other machine learning models to offer more accurate predictions in the stock market. In addition, these models have the ability to capture the subtleties of human language better than other text-modelling approaches. The numerous sophisticated models linking language and businesses are trained on large corpora of business text, but they lack the capability of understanding the most recent company filings, estimates, and their quarterly developments. Consequently, these shortcomings of the models affect the possibility of subsequent corporate market responses, as well as the development, behavior, and duration of the stock market and decimal acquisition price of commodities and goods.

Trends in Journalism

We do know that the economics of journalism have to change because many of the old cobblers are disappearing. We know that substantial and comprehensive investigative journalism can be highly popular. There is abundant evidence to support the view if journalism is well-funded and well-conceived, it can be and is extraordinarily popular with readers. Public broadcasters across the world have considerable evidence to back up this simple point. People do wish to be informed. They do not want to be misled. The question is whether this demand can be satisfied within an entirely new economic model, or whether new economic models need to be found and developed.

News organizations around the world are changing rapidly. The old economics of the news industry is dying, or at least one part of it is dying - media ownership that relies for the bulk of its profits on advertising. What is emerging is unclear. A key issue that the owners and managers of media organizations are grappling with is how to finance the making of news. Will the dominant model be a subscription-based model, under which content is sold to readers with real regard for the quality of that content? Or will ownership of media organizations that lose money or make a modest profit be seen primarily as a public relations device in order to produce good advertising rates? The blunt answer is that no one knows.

CHAPTER 9

Conclusion and Recap of Key Learnings

In conclusion, we echo the following piece of advice from Gordon Gekko (Michael Douglas from Wall Street): "The most valuable commodity I know of is information." Truth be told, we do live in a world of information overload, and sorting out the essential from the non-essential often seems to require effort, skill, and patience. Clearly, not everything that glitters is gold, and recognizing what is what, and how to use it to one's advantage constitutes the essence of "information management." It's been a tough 13 weeks, but now you know how! We are so very proud of you! Enjoy the tasting of your spicy financial curry! We will close our guide by noting that we have tried our best to motivate, inspire, inform, and enlighten you. As always, your opinions, suggestions, and comments are greatly appreciated. Thank you for listening!

In this chapter, we try to help you put it all together by rehashing and summarizing all the key takeaways, and subtly encouraging you to develop an inquiring and healthy sense of skepticism. In the process, we introduce and discuss "The Fractal Model of Financial

News," by which we mean that the underlying principles of our news analysis approach, derived from experience and intuition, bear similarities with the underlying principles of the similar market analysis models used by many practitioners in the real world. The chapter answers the repeatedly asked questions in course evaluations. Finally, the chapter provides the project details and the deliverables for the project designed to complete the learning experience!

www.ingramcontent.com/pod-product-compliance
Lightning Source LLC
LaVergne TN
LVHW100104250926
848814LV00045B/20
* 9 7 9 8 3 3 0 3 1 7 8 0 6 *